Celtic Guitar
─ by Doc Rossi ─

An Approach to Playing Traditional Dance Music on the Guitar

ISBN 978-1 57424-266-9
SAN 683-8022

Cover by James Creative Group

This book is dedicated to the traditional musicians who have helped me learn to play their music - Lucy Farr, Tommy Healy, Jimmy Power, Bob Cann, Dan Quinn, Roger Digby, and The Rakes: Paul Gross, Michael Plunkett and Reg Hall.

Cover photo by Adrian Frearson

Contents

Introduction

If you look through the titles of the tunes in this book, you'll see that most of them come from Irish traditional music. Irish music has had an enormous influence on the revival of traditional musics of Western cultures, thanks to pioneering groups like The Chieftains, Planxty, The Bothy Band, De Dannan, and a host of others. The energy and drive of Irish traditional music and the success of popular bands who have brought it to a wider audience have inspired musicians from other countries and cultures to take the traditional music of their own culture to a different level. A prime example is Alan Stivell, who spearheaded a revival of Breton music with his *Renaissance of the Celtic Harp*. Another is Ale Möller and his work with Scandinavian traditional music. Today we can enjoy a variety of "Celtic" music from all over Europe and North America because "Celtic" has become a style or aesthetic approach as much as anything else.

I concentrate on Irish tunes in this book because Irish traditional music is so well known and appreciated, and also because it has a highly evolved style of ornamentation and variation. I've also included some tunes from other countries and cultures not just because they're great tunes, but to help you understand how what you learn in one style of music can be carried over into another without blurring the differences into some nondescript mix. What I'm working on is a style of guitar playing that respects the traditions that the music comes from while making the most of the idiomatic characteristics of the guitar itself.

There are a lot of great guitarists playing traditional music of all kinds, using a variety of tunings from standard to Dropped-D, DADGAD and loads of others, and I've tried them all. I've always been fascinated by the different sounds different tunings allow, but I don't want to be changing tunings all the time, nor do I want to be moving a capo up and down the neck with each key change, at least not when I'm performing. This has led me to look at more practical issues, like how adaptable a tuning is to playing in several keys, how easy and intuitive the fingerings are, and more importantly than anything else, whether a tuning actually helps the flow and feel of the music. The tuning I use in this book might seem a little unusual at first, but for me, it meets all the criteria.

The tuning I use is C F C G C F, from low to high. Using a capo at the second fret gives D G D A D G. Notice that the top four strings use the same intervals as the lower four in Dropped-D and DADGAD. In fact, I devised this tuning when I discovered how well the music flowed when I played tunes on the lower strings in those tunings. I found, however, that playing the tune two octaves below the fiddle, flute and other traditional instruments wasn't ideal, and I missed the low G found on tenor banjo and fiddle. In the end, I found that the combination of the fifths and fourths - a cross between fiddle and guitar - made it easy to play tunes in all the important traditional keys or modes without moving the capo or having to negotiate difficult position shifts, while at the same time providing a number of open strings and other possibilities for accompanying myself and others. It is also a good tuning for playing chords, bass lines and counter-melodies. I would suggest using light top, heavy bottom strings.

This book is primarily about melody playing with a flatpick, so I don't talk about accompaniment beyond including some very basic chords. Traditional music is often drone-based and modal rather than based on a system of major and minor keys. It is my feeling that to play good backup you have to know the tunes, so take this book as a first step - learn the tunes, then learn to accompany them. Basic chord shapes are given in the appendix, but I don't want to encourage banging out the chords behind the tunes! Accompaniment is a very subtle art. The most important advice I can give about backing up is to listen to whom you're playing with and don't swamp them.

The tablature follows normal conventions: the top line represents the top or highest-pitched string; the lower represents the sixth or lowest string; numbers represent frets, with 0 being an open string. The rhythm markings are the same as those used in standard guitar notation, meaning that it is slightly simplified to make it easier to read, so you should let some notes ring on longer than indicated. A tie or slur between notes of different pitches indicates that the first note is sounded with the pick, with the note or notes following being hammer-ons, pull-offs or slides. Some slides are also marked with an S. I haven't marked the places where I bend one note into another. I often do this when going from a fretted note to an open one, for example, from f# on the second string to the top g. Two parallel slashes in the final measure of a tune means that the tune ends on the note just before them. Grace notes are smaller than main notes and can be left out when you are first learning a tune. In Part One I provide two versions of a tune in order to illustrate the basics of ornamentation. In the rest of the book, ornamentation and variations are indicated by lower-case letters above the measure that refer to the alternate measures at the end of the piece. The last three pieces in the book are duets.

In addition to tablature, I've included notation for anyone who would like to play these tunes in a different tuning. The notation doesn't include left-hand fingerings, but it does include all of the ornaments.

PART ONE
Basic Technique & Ornamentation

I use a rather stiff yet thin flatpick - a Tortex .60 (orange) - and I often use the rounded edge rather than the point. I find this gives me a fuller tone and that the pick glides over the strings more easily. I adjust my grip to make the flatpick more or less flexible as needed. I try to keep my right wrist as loose as possible and in general use an up-and-down motion, except when playing jigs, which are discussed later. My right-hand fingers very lightly touch the top and I occasionally rest my wrist or forearm on the bridge, but in general I try to keep my wrist as free as possible.

For the left hand, the second fret is "home" - that is, the index finger hovers over the second fret, going down to the first only when necessary. The middle, ring and little finger cover frets three, four and five respectively, but I often find that I want to use a stronger finger on the fourth or fifth fret, especially when there is an ornament involved, so I move my left hand up the neck and fret with the middle or ring finger - whatever feels most comfortable and solid.

Traditional music is primarily oral, but many traditional players do take tunes from tune books. Most printed sources give rather bare settings of the tunes with little or no ornamentation indicated, and it is up to the players to bring them to life and make them their own. In this first section we look at the basic ornaments as they might be played in some well-known tunes. All of the ornamentation in this section is written out in full. In Part Two and Part Three, several ornaments are included in the tab and notation, while others are given at the end of the piece in alternate measures. Ornamentation in traditional music is improvised and spontaneous. I try to show you which ornaments might be played where, but these arrangements are not written in stone: they simply illustrate different ways of gracing notes based on what I've learned from the musicians who taught me.

Ornamentation and variation are very important in Irish traditional music, and each instrument has its own idiomatic ornaments. Since the guitar is a relative newcomer, the door is open for us to discover which ornaments suit it best, but we can and should learn from traditional players on other instruments. The obvious choice might be the banjo, and a lot can be learned from traditional banjo players, but the banjo and the guitar are also very different in terms of attack, sustain, tone, tension and stringing. It is important to listen to all of the main traditional instruments to understand the intricacies of ornamentation and variation, then apply what you learn to the guitar.

Most ornaments on the guitar are played using hammer-ons, pull-offs, or slides. They should be played quickly, without putting the other notes in the bar out of time. In other words, they "borrow" time from the notes near them. Don't dwell too long on the ornaments - they are really just a flick of a left-hand finger or two and should add bounce and lightness. The exception to this is the plucked triplet, which is primarily a right-hand ornament. They should also be played light and bouncy; they sometimes have a more percussive or rhythmic rather than melodic effect.

Here is a brief rundown of what the ornaments look like on paper. You can hear them in context on the CD.

A single grace note or *acciaccatura* is written as a small eighth note with a line through its stem. They are often placed between notes of the same pitch, or before an important note to give it more emphasis. Pick the grace and pull off for the main note.

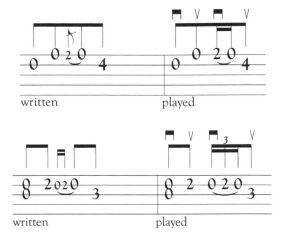

Double grace notes or trills are written as two sixteenth notes. Pick the first note, then quickly hammer-on and pull-off the next two.

Triplets are three notes played in the place of two. There are several kinds - plucked, slurred, ascending and descending. They are often shown in tune books, but are also used to decorate quarter notes or to fill in between notes that are more than a step apart.

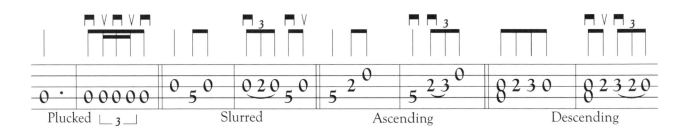

Rolls or turns are four- or five-note ornaments that use the notes just above and below the main note. Often played as triplets on plucked instruments, they are used to decorate quarter notes and dotted quarter notes, or a group of quarter and eighth notes of the same pitch.

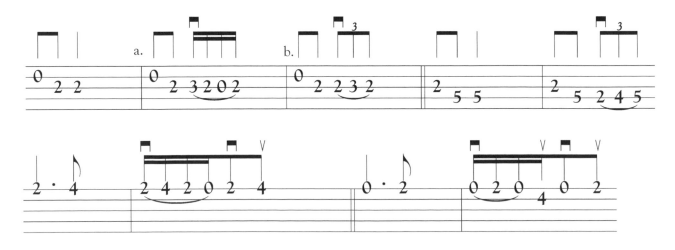

Cranning or popping is a technique used by pipers on the low D or E. It is played by lifting off single fingers in quick succession to achieve a bubbling effect. We can imitate this on the guitar by using a quick succession of one hammer-on and two pull-offs.

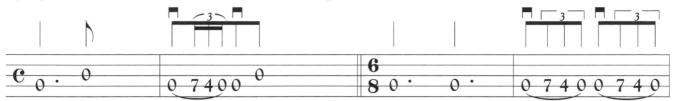

The guitar has a lot of sustain, so a note ringing on without any added ornamentation can be very effective, as can adding harmony notes or chords. Keep in mind that ornamentation can be overdone. Silence and space are often overlooked elements of tasteful playing.

NOTES ON INDIVIDUAL TUNES

We start off with The Peacock's Feather and The Fairies' Hornpipe. The Fairies' is made up of three strands - measures 1-4, 5-8 and 9-12. Measures 13-16 are the same as 5-8, but note the descending triplet in measure 15 - this is a typical ornament or variation. The Peacock's Feather has a similar structure and several descending triplets.

Next up are a pair of jigs. There are different ways to pick jigs; the two most common I've seen traditional banjo players use are down-up-down/down-up-down and down-up-down/up-down-up, with string crossings sometimes breaking the pattern. I favor the first pattern because I like the drive it naturally has, but it does have the awkward feature of consecutive downstrokes, which can sometimes be tricky in quick tunes. In addition to adding more drive and interest, ornaments can also make a tricky passage easier to play by breaking the picking pattern with hammer-ons, pull-offs or plucked triplets, which in jigs look like this:

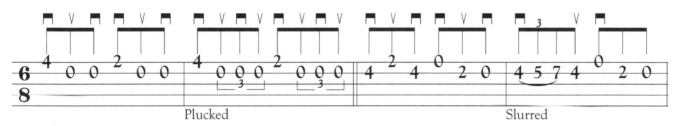

I learned The Humours of Kilcogher from piper and pipe maker Didier Heuline; my arrangement uses plucked triplets in several measures, crans in measures 3 and 4, and a harmonic variation in measures 11-12 which I play the last time through. I learned The Cordal Jig from The Rakes - Reg Hall (melodeon and piano), Michael Plunket (fiddle and flute) and Paul Gross (fiddle and piano), who were often joined by Ron Somers (drums), Lucy Farr (fiddle) and Tommy Healy (flute). The Cordal Jig, or Julia Clifford's, shows different ways of playing a dotted quarter note in measures 1, 5 and 17. The quarter notes throughout the tune can be played as trills, rolls or triplets; the one in measure 7 is perfect for an ascending triplet. Measures 2 and 15 show typical variations.

The Long Note may be the only tune whose name actually describes a musical characteristic of the tune itself. The variations in the second version show several ways of playing dotted quarter notes. These would normally be rolled except that the main note is the middle open D where a real roll isn't possible, so instead I use sliding into a unison, hammering on to a unison, plucked triplets, and a cran. Other ornaments in this setting include triplets and rolls replacing quarter notes, plus single and double graces.

I learned Rodney's Glory - a set dance that is often played as a hornpipe or reel - from Martin Byrnes's excellent Leader LP. He uses a lot of ornamentation in his elegant, lilting style.

The Peacock's Feather

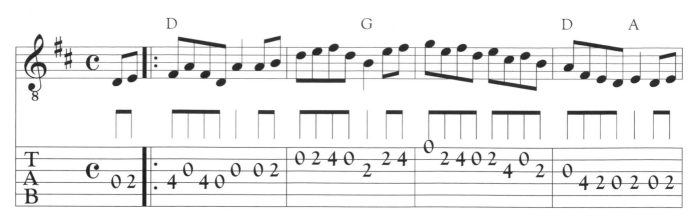

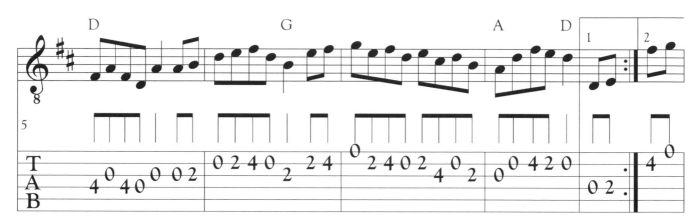

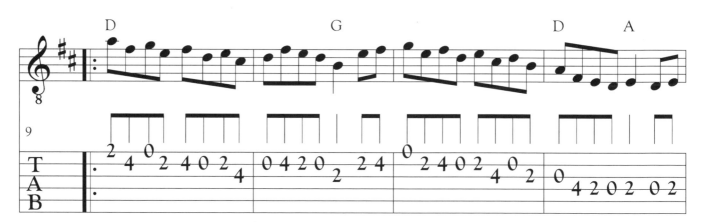

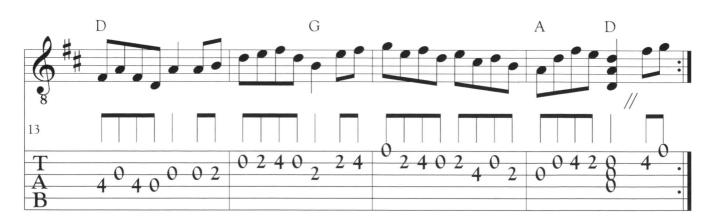

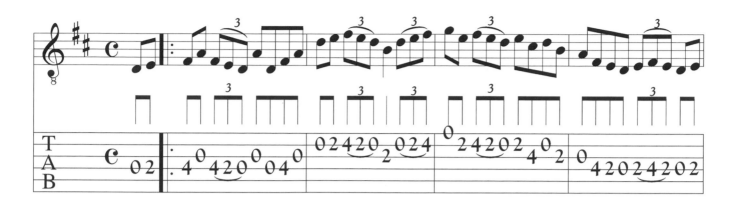

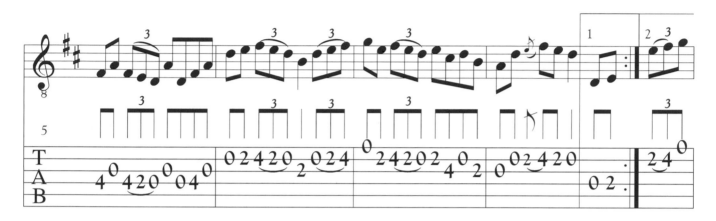

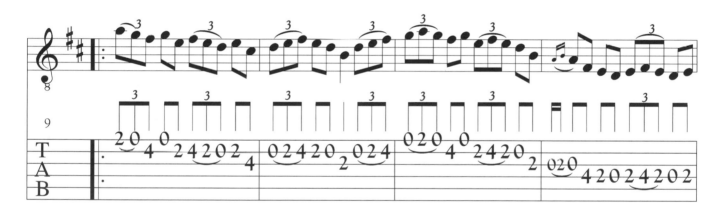

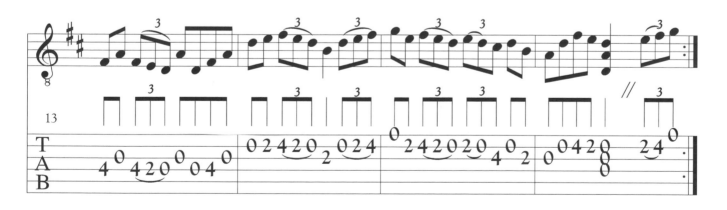

9

The Fairies' Hornpipe

11

The Humours of Kilcogher

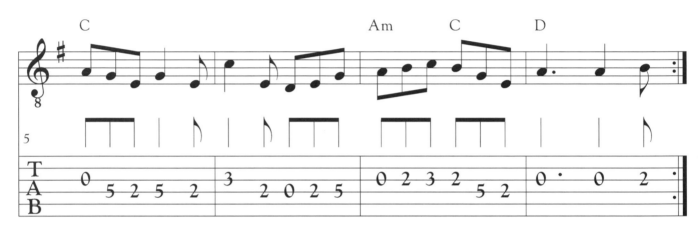

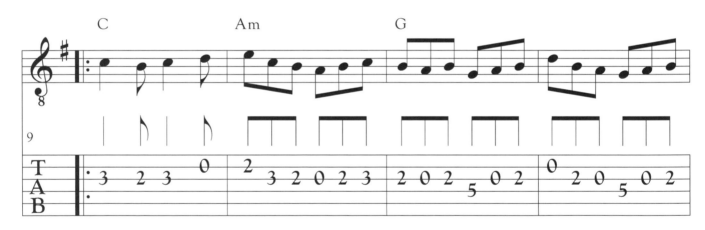

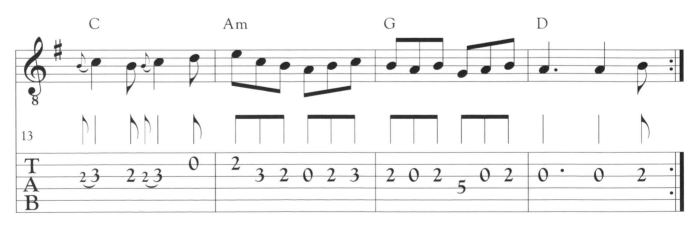

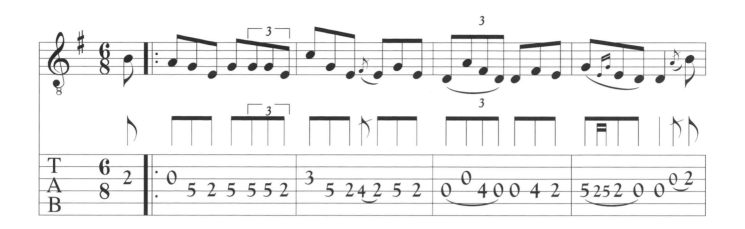

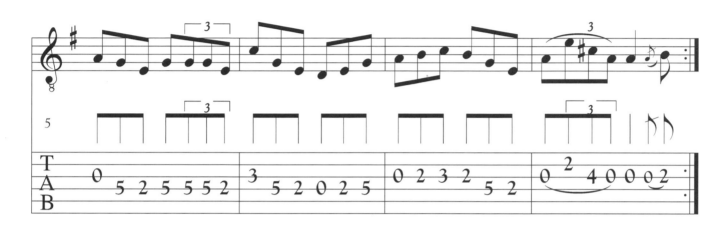

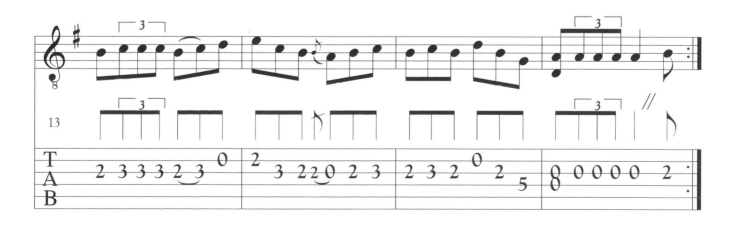

The Cordal Jig

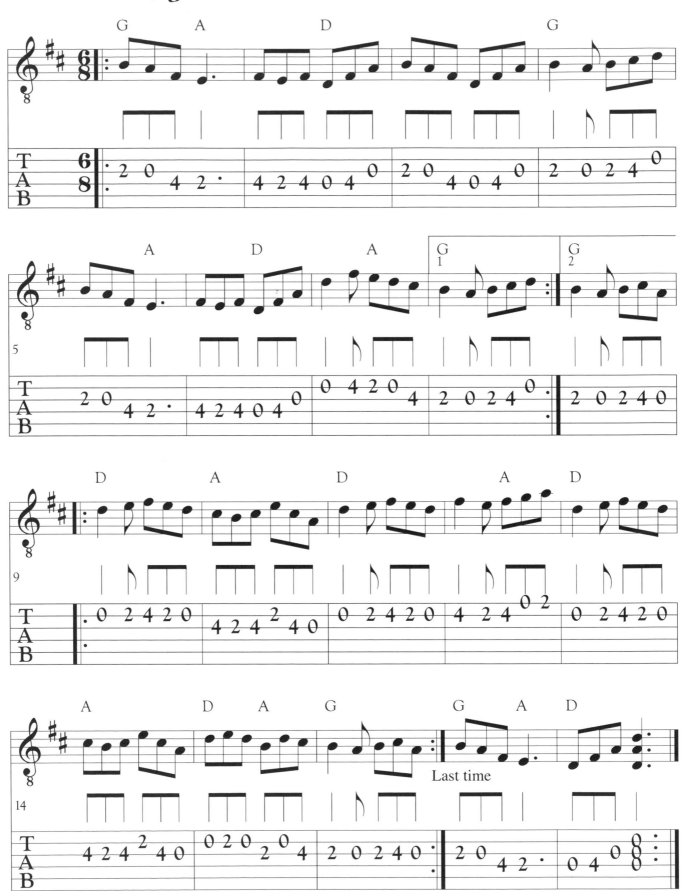

14

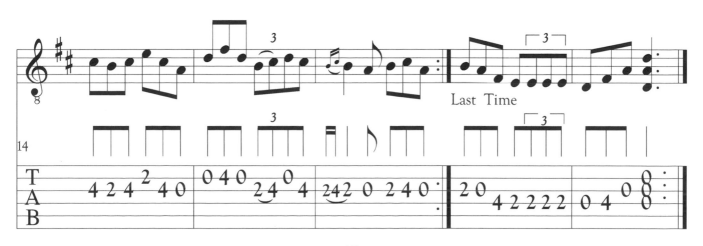

Last Time

15

The Long Note

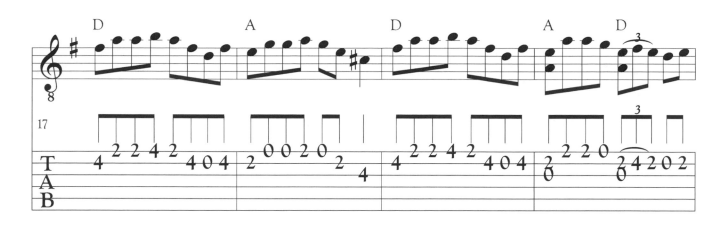

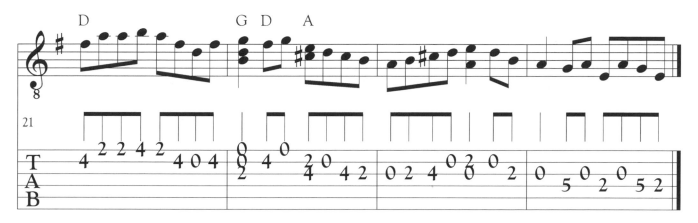

VERSION TWO

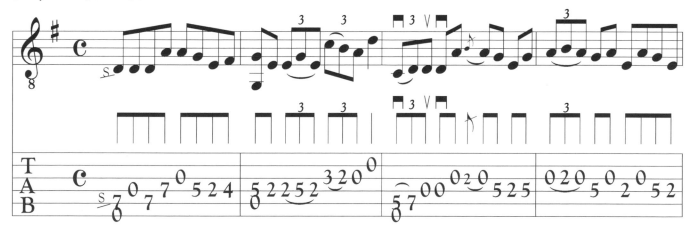

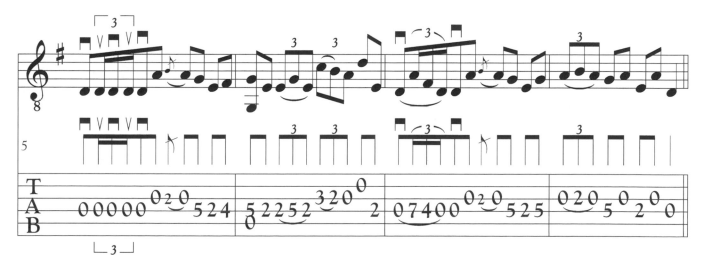

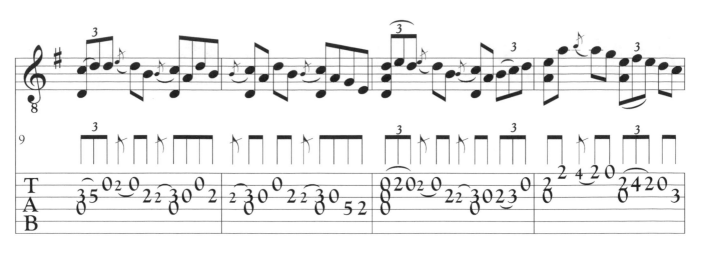

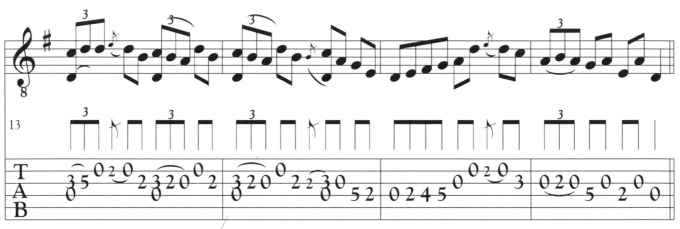

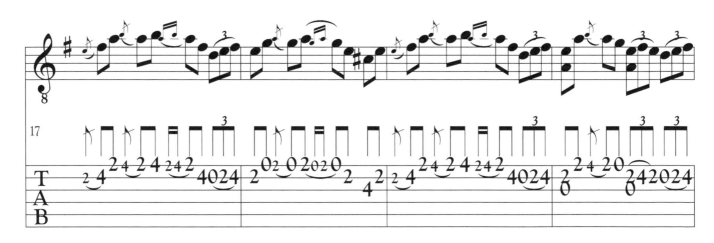

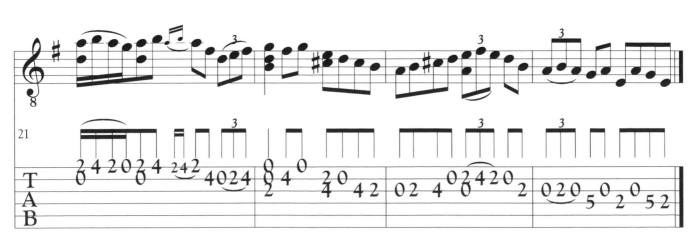

Rodney's Glory

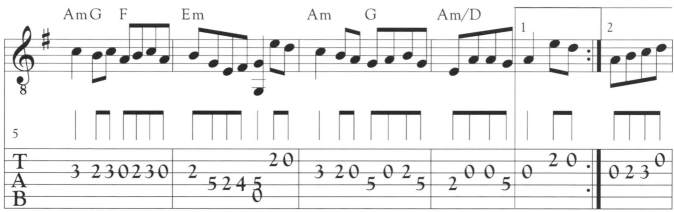

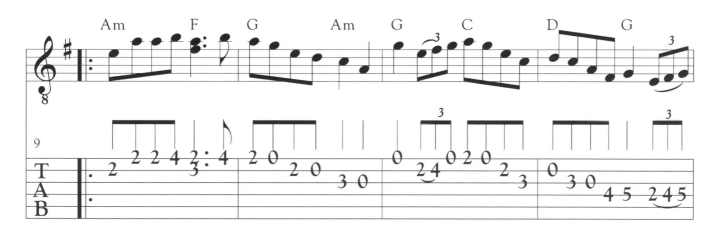

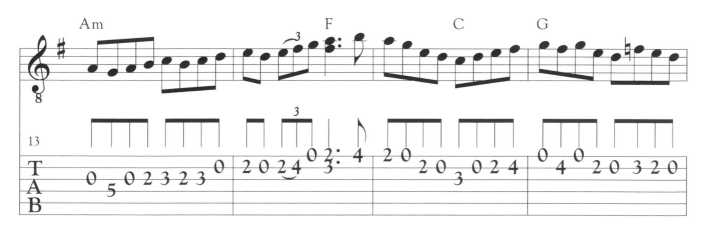

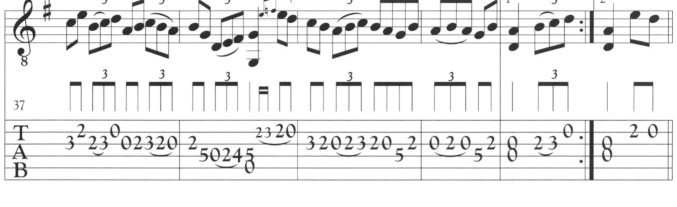

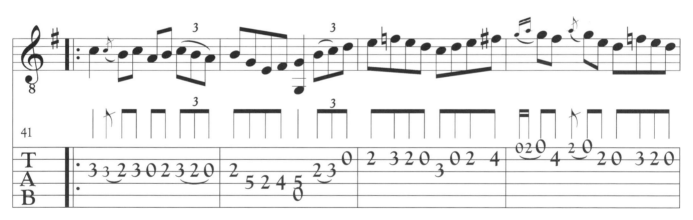

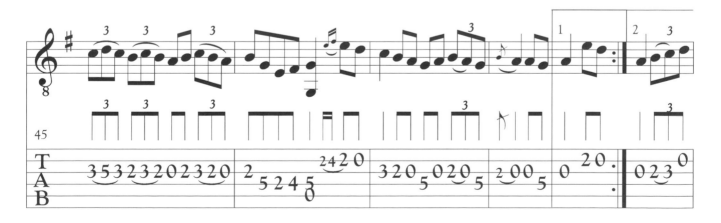

PART TWO
A Selection of Irish Tunes

Jigs

Brian O'Lynn is another fine, driving tune from Martin Byrnes. Note the single graces on the first notes of measures 1, 3, 5, 7 and 15, and the triplets in the alternate measures at the end. A Trip to Athlone and The Mist Covered Mountain are popular session tunes. They have several instances of plucked triplets, as well as several single graces.

Brian O'Lynn

23

A Trip to Athlone

The Mist Covered Mountain

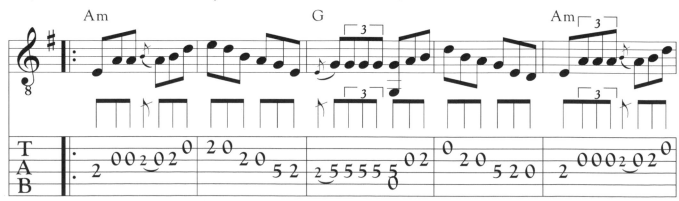

The Mooncoin is a three-part jig in A mixolydian, easy enough to play if not taken too quickly. Note measures 1 and 5, and 9 and 13 - I use plucked triplets to break up the standard picking pattern, effectively avoiding consecutive downstrokes. There are also plenty of single graces between consecutive notes of the same pitch.

The Lark in the Morning is a popular four-part jig in D. As with The Mooncoin, there are plenty of plucked triplets and single graces. I've written out alternative endings which can be substituted for any of the others: a single grace note in measure 16 and a plucked triplet in measure 24. I don't necessarily play this as written - these are just some ideas for you to try.

The Mooncoin Jig

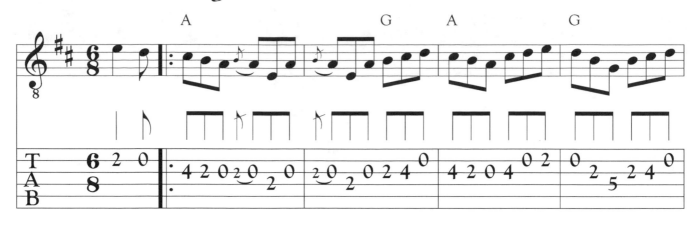

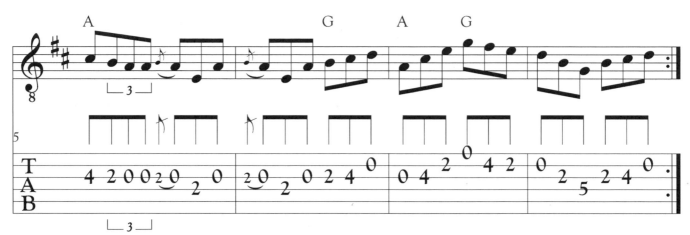

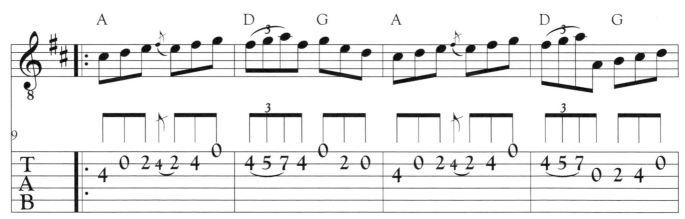

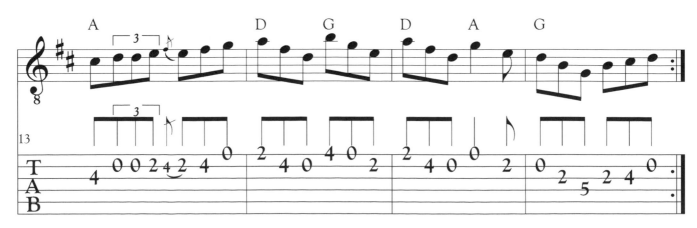

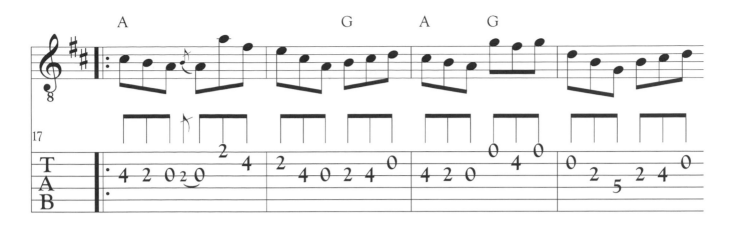

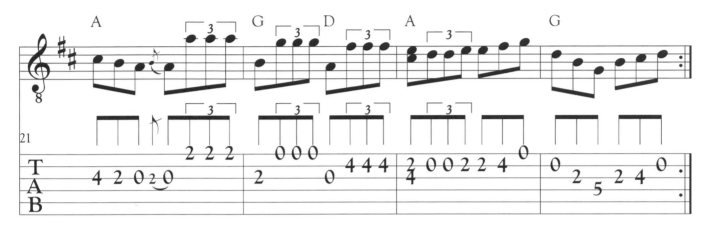

The Lark in the Morning

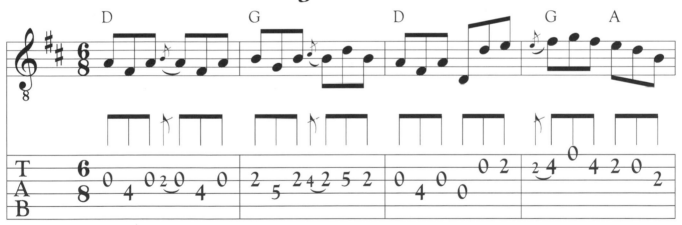

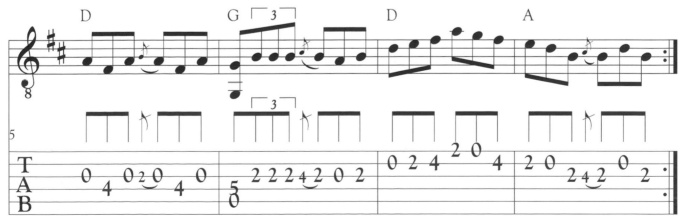

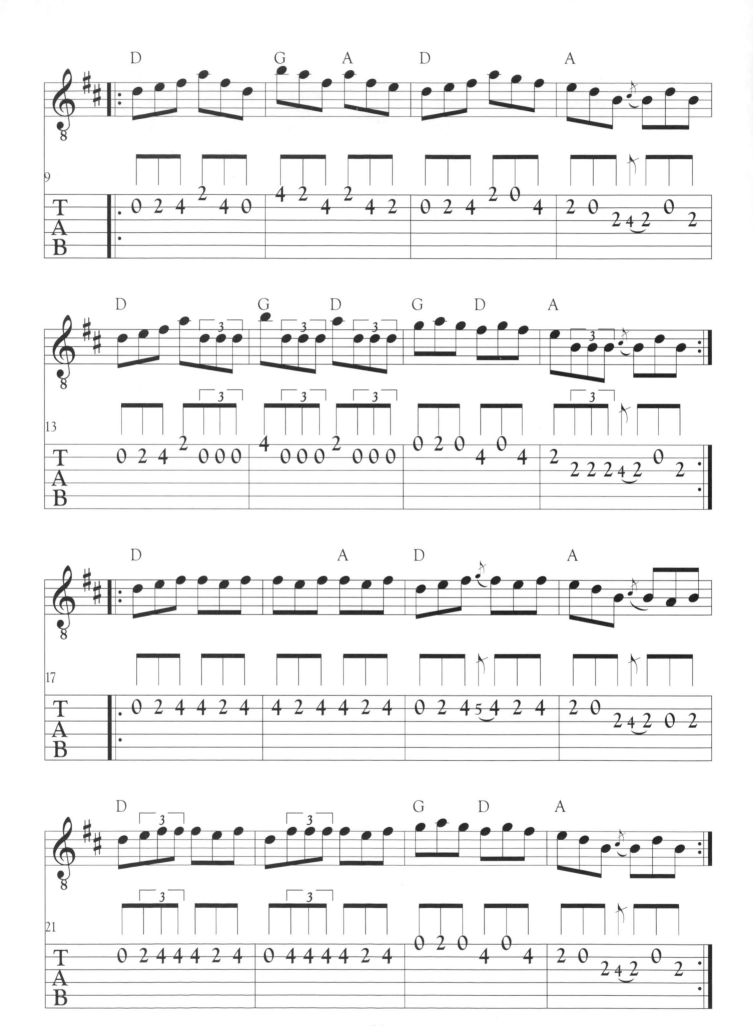

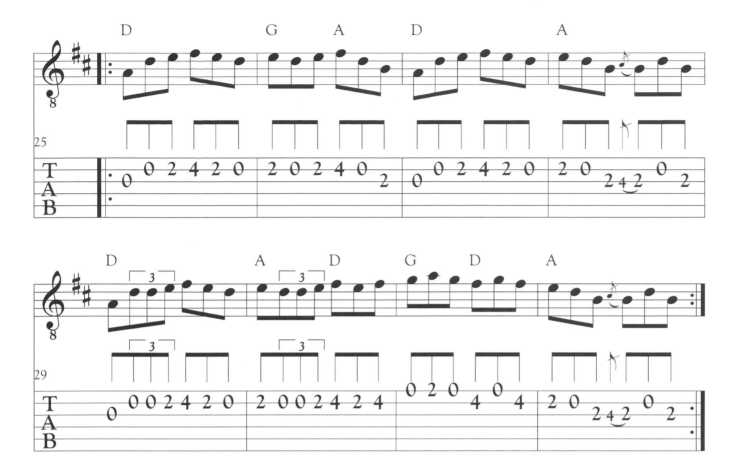

The Swallow Tail is a popular session tune in Em. Its chief difficulty is barring across two or three strings to maintain a drone on E. The Banks of Lough Gowna is in Bm. There are several ways of ornamenting the repeated notes in measures 1 and 5 and the dotted quarters in measures 9 and 13.

An Phis Fhliuch is a classic slip jig from the piping of Willy Clancy. Slip jigs and hop jigs are in 9/8 time - three beats per measure with the dotted quarter having one beat. I learned this tune off one of Willy Clancy's Topic recordings and have tried to adapt some of his ornaments and variations to the guitar.

The Rakes in 1986. Clockwise from left, Michael Plunkett, Ron Somers, Reg Hall, Hugh Rippon (caller), Paul Gross, Lucy Farr, Tommy Healy.

The Swallow Tail Jig

30

The Banks of Lough Gowna

31

An Phis Fhliuch

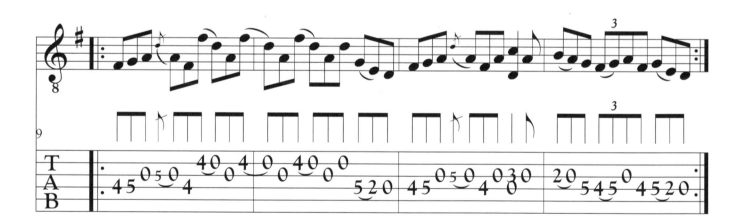

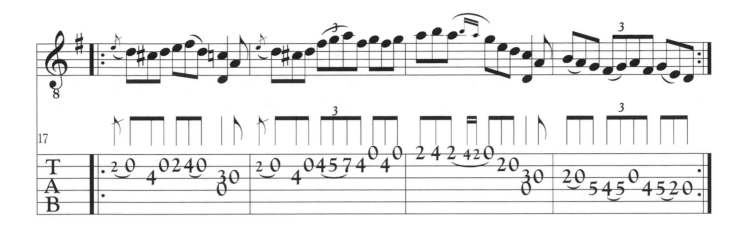

hornpipes & set dances

Poll Ha'penny dates from at least the 18th century. Apparently Turlough O'Carolan liked this tune so much that he said he would rather have written it more than any of his own tunes.

I learned The Cliff and The Galway from Reg Hall, who plays them on the G/D melodeon. Ornaments in The Cliff include a triplet in measure 8, and a descending triplet in measure 16. Notice that the first half of measures 10 and 11 are the same except that the latter includes a descending triplet. Reg plays measures 1 and 5 as in the variation, but other versions have the D on the third beat, which is easier to play, especially when you're starting out. I've included more ornaments in the alternate version of measures 9-12. There are similar variations for The Galway, including two ways of decorating a middle G (variations a and b), and two ways to add triplets. To play the triplet in b, I slide the index finger up to the fourth fret.

I learned the Greencastle and Liverpool hornpipes from the great Anglo concertina player Roger Digby. Roger plays the Greencastle as given here, and I've included an alternate B part that I've heard others play. This tune is played as often in D as it is in G. In the Liverpool, the last four measures of each part are the same, so the B part shows variations you can use, while the recording demonstrates others.

The first version of The Princess Royal (measures 1-20) is often attributed to O'Carolan. I learned the other version from Michael Plunkett and Paul Gross of The Rakes; they in turn had it from two of the McCusker brothers, who recorded it live for the BBC on unison fiddles. My arrangement of the Blackbird is based on Martin Byrnes' setting. He played it with Rodney's Glory.

Poll Ha'penny

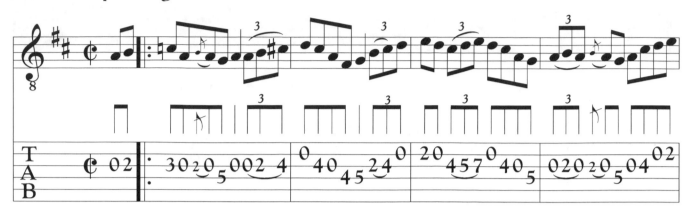

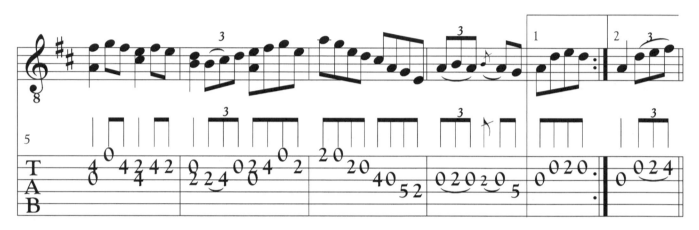

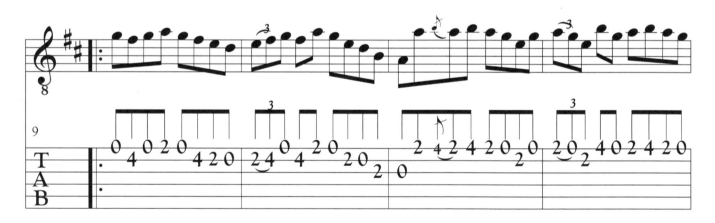

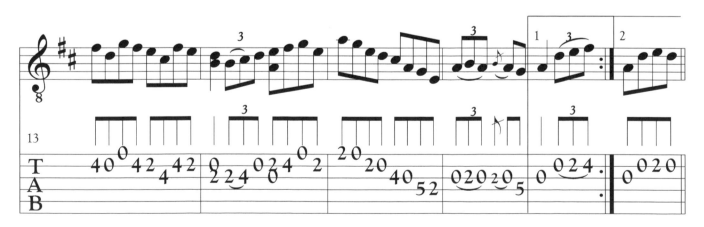

The Princess Royal

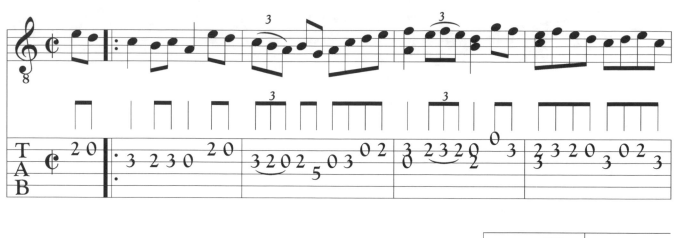

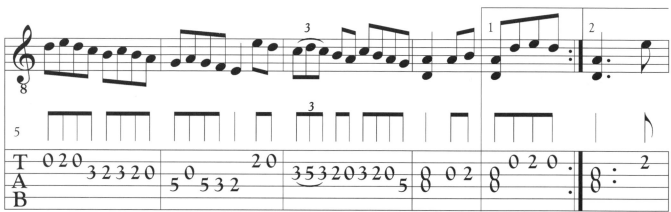

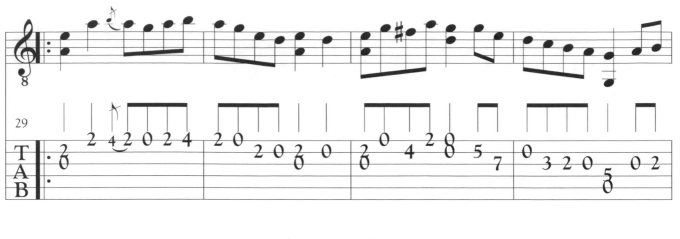

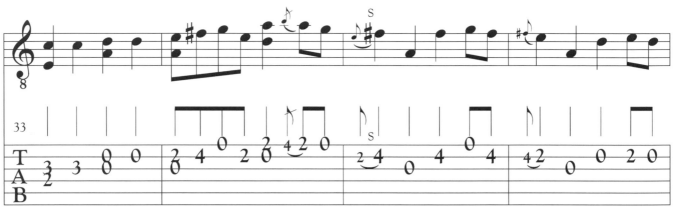

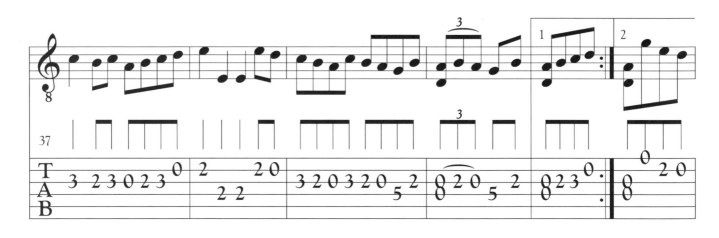

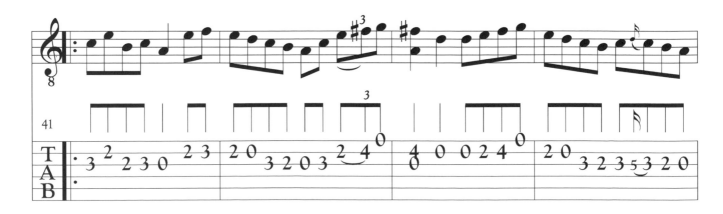

The Blackbird

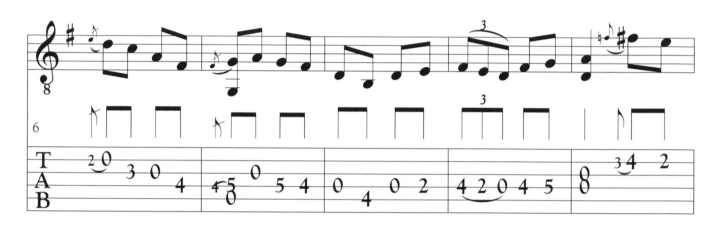

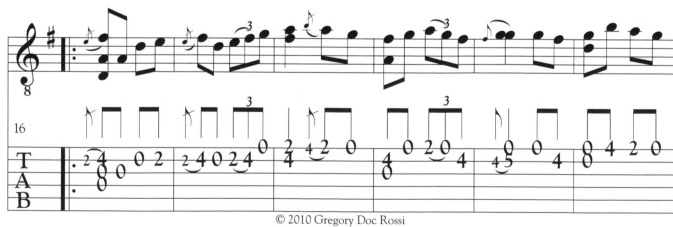

42

43

The Cliff

44

The Galway

The Greencastle Hornpipe

46

The Liverpool Hornpipe

Alternate B music for Greencastle Hornpipe

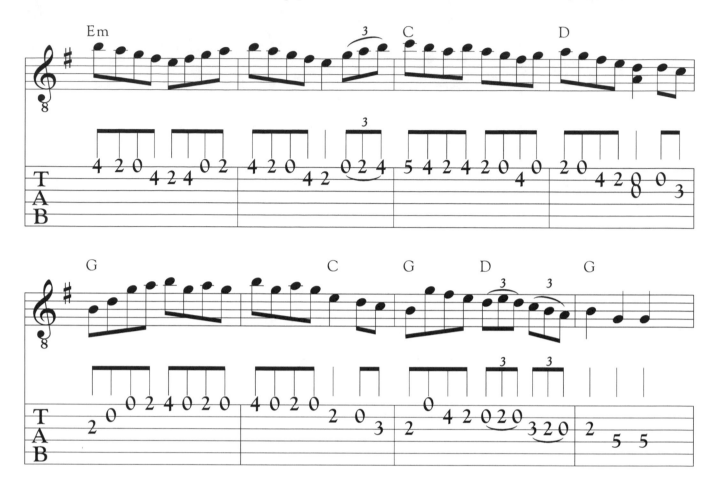

reels

The Flowers of Edinburgh is very well known as both a hornpipe and a reel. The Flowers of Michigan is a rare tune with some similarities to the Jug of Punch and The Temperance Reel, which Tommy Healy and I used to play together whenever we had the chance.

Tommy Peoples and De Danann have recorded The Woman of the House; De Danann, play it with The Log Cabin, a great reel that has been recorded many times. I learned The Virginia from The Rakes.

The final medley of reels comes from The McCusker brothers, a nine-piece ceildh band that recorded them at break neck speed back in the 1950s. I think The Traveler's shows just how useful the top G course can be - I bounce off of it quite a lot in this tune and in Miss Thorton's. It helps me build up the momentum and lets me syncopate things a bit more easily. I give an alternative way of playing the B part of Miss Thorton's that gives a more open sound. I also give an alternate B part for The Scholar that is not traditional. The usual chords here would be D and C, but moving the lower line down chromatically adds a different dimension to the tune the second time around.

The Flowers of Edinburgh

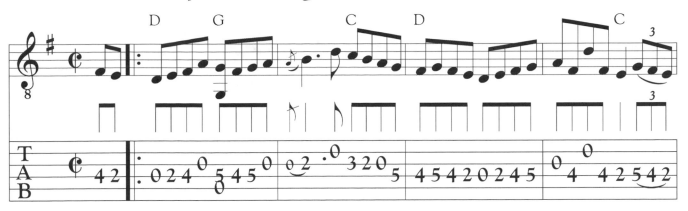

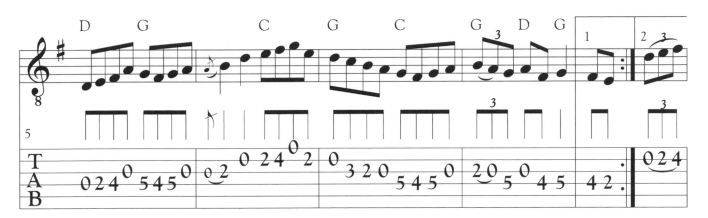

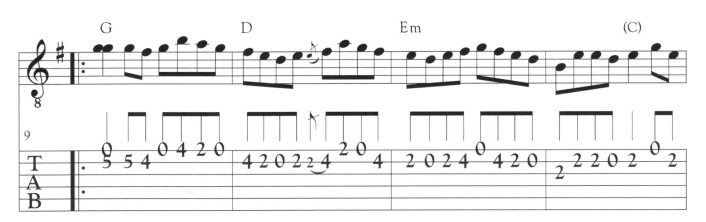

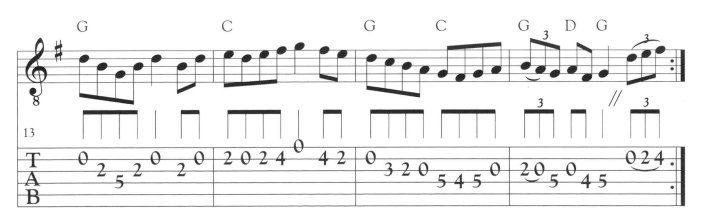

The Flowers of Michigan

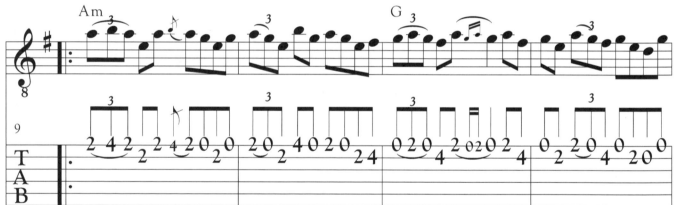

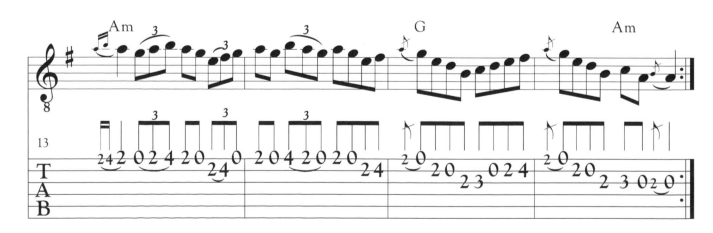

The Temperance

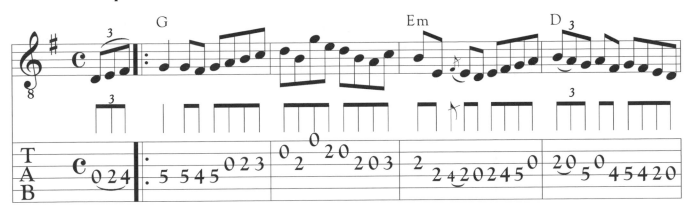

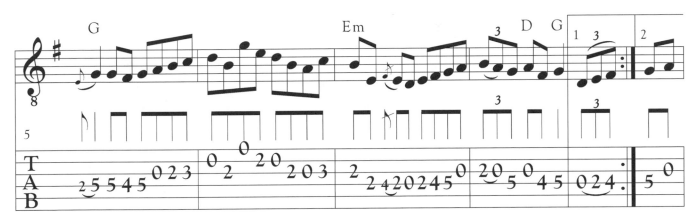

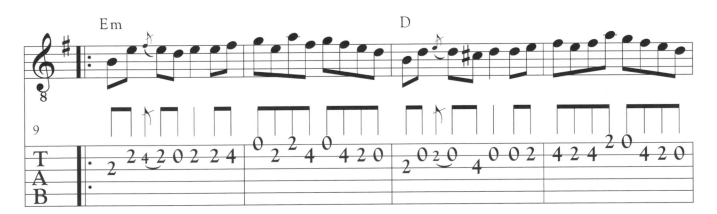

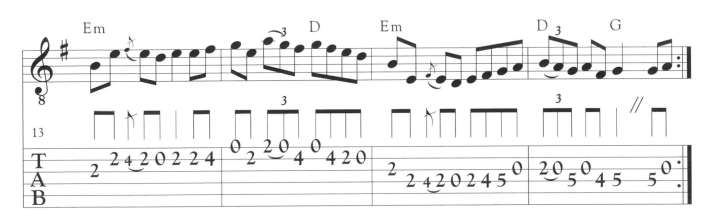

The Woman of the House

The Log Cabin

The Virginia

The Traveler's

The Scholar

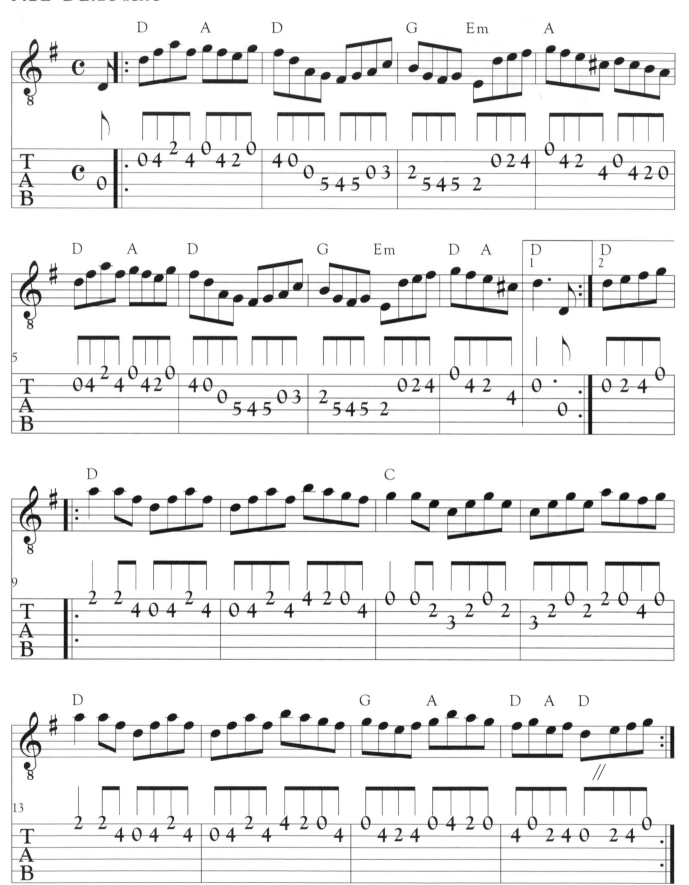

Miss Thorton's

Alternate B music for The Scholar

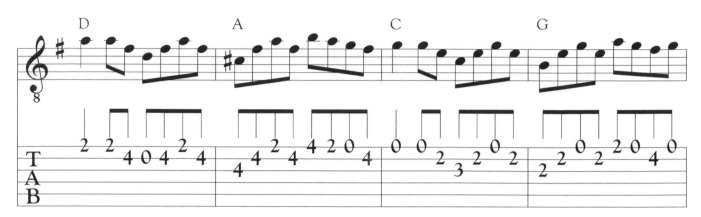

Alternate fingering for B music of Miss Thorton's

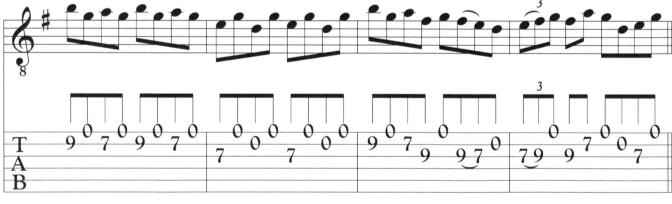

part three
Tunes from other Cultures

I first heard French-Canadian music through recordings of Louis Beaudoin and of the Richlieu family. There is a tradition of playing what they call crooked tunes, or tunes with an uneven number of measures and/or unexpected phrasing, just to keep the dancers alert. Although usually played as a single tune, this piece is actually made up of two tunes - La Cardeuse and Le Triomphe. There have been several recordings of them with the parts arranged in different ways. I like to play this medley AA BB AC DD EE, repeat it, then finish with the A music. On the CD I use a type of cross picking for the quarter notes in section B, outlining the chords with a triplet feel.

Jockey to the Fair dates from the 18th century. It comes in several versions and is found in England as a Morris dance as well as in Ireland as a set dance. It sits well on the guitar as a solo piece, especially if you hold on to the chords to create the suspensions so often found in baroque music. I've teamed it up with a couple of English jigs. The Flaxley Green Dance dates from about the same period, and is associated with fiddler and wheelwright William Henry Robinson from the village of Abbots Bromley, which, like Flaxley Green, is in Staffordshire. Tom Jones was very popular in the 18th century, appearing in several mid-century tune books after the publication of Henry Fielding's famous novel. It's normally played in D, but I've set it in G to make the best use of the chords available in that key.

Foul Weather Call and The Dorsetshire Hornpipe are English tunes that I play as Schottisches. I learned Foul Weather Call from Dan Quinn - a really fine melodeon player - and Roger Digby. The first time through is pretty much the basic melody; the second time I develop a way of self-accompanying the tune. I often play this with right-hand damping. I may well have learned The Dorsetshire Hornpipe from Dan and Roger, too - or maybe from that grand institution of trad, Osmosis.

American Old Time music owes a lot to Irish and Scottish music, but has a character all its own. I learned this version of Polly Put the Kettle On from banjo player David Murphy. I play it with a lot of swing and let the drones ring as much as possible.

We finish with three duets. The first is my arrangement of a four-part jig from *Cent Contredanses en Rond*, by Robert Daubat, published in Ghent, Belgium in 1757. Daubat's fascinating collection is almost like a missing link between baroque and traditional music. My band Góntia specializes in the music. Mantovana is a very old tune that may come from the Italian city of Mantova, but I learned it in French sessions. I've written a second part to go with it. Girandula is a traditional Corsican tune usually played in Gm. You can also play it in Gm in this tuning, but I prefer it in Dm for the drones. As with Mantovana, I have provided a harmony part. The order is AA BB CC AA.

La Cardeuse & Le Triomphe

Jockey to the Fair

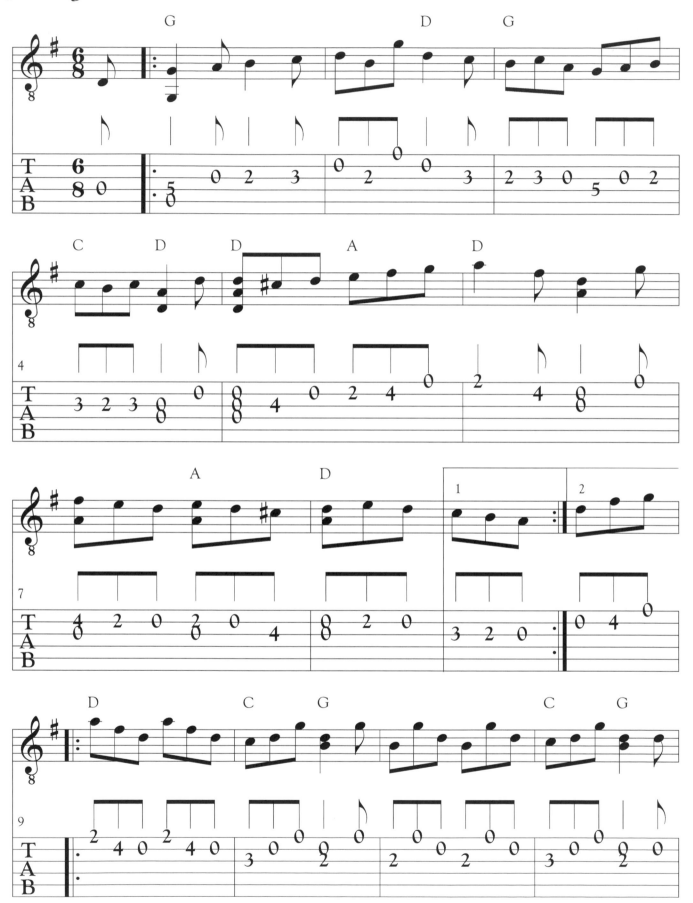

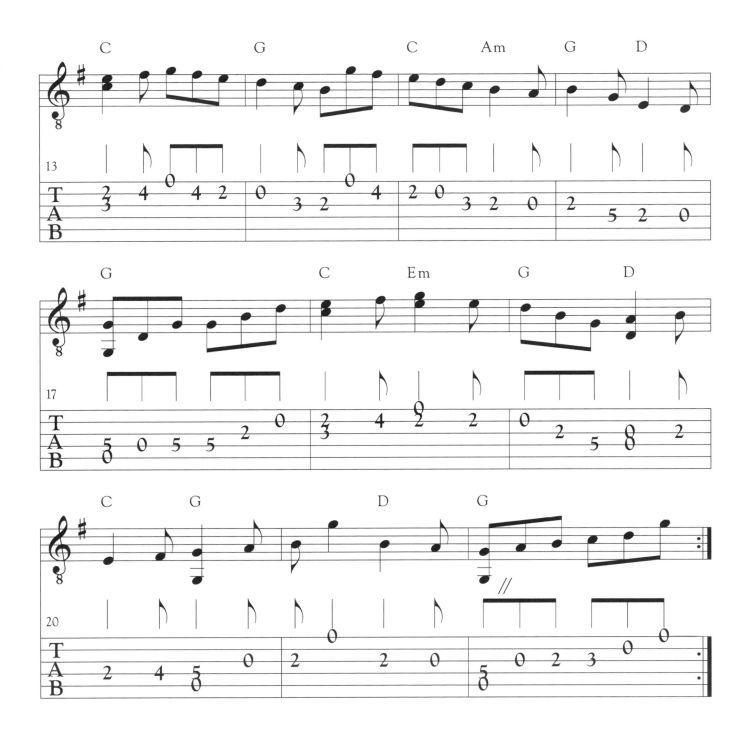

The Flaxley Green Dance

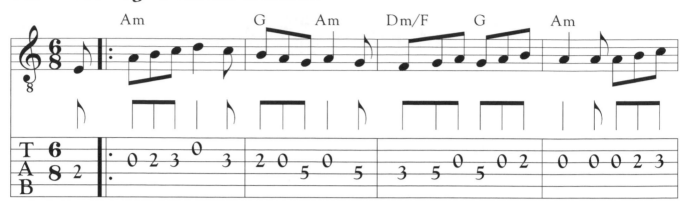

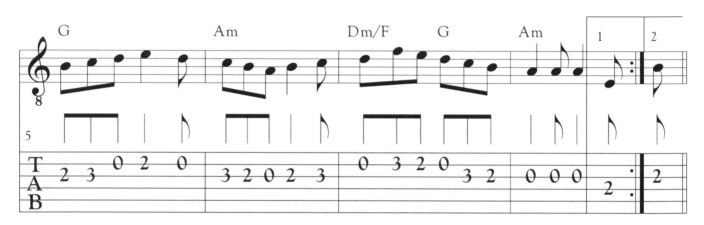

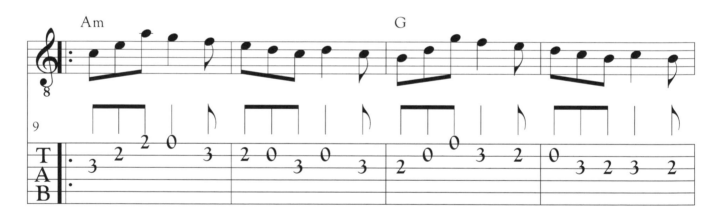

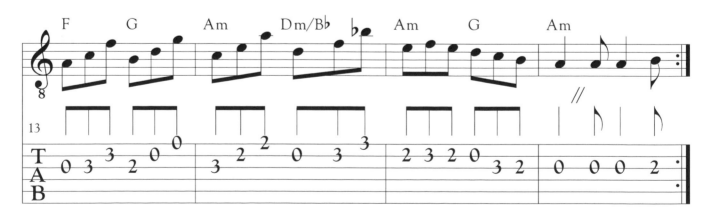

Tom Jones

Foul Weather Call

The Dorsetshire Hornpipe

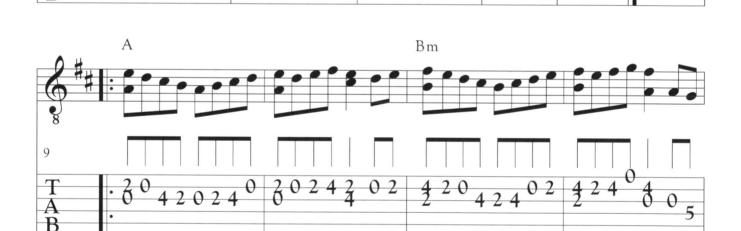

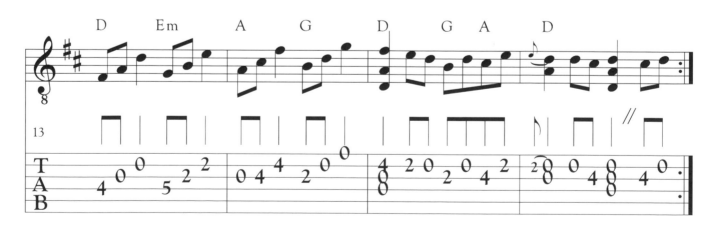

Polly put the Kettle On

Le Concert ou La Sabatine - Part One

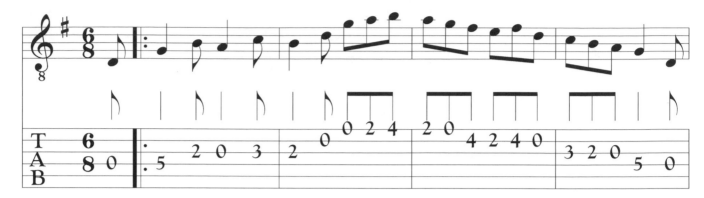

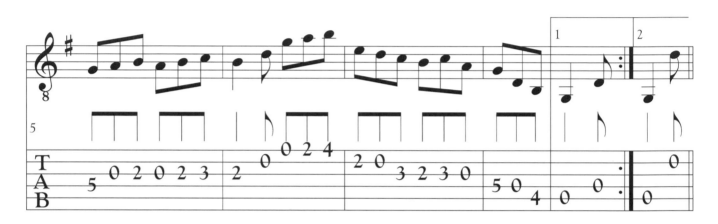

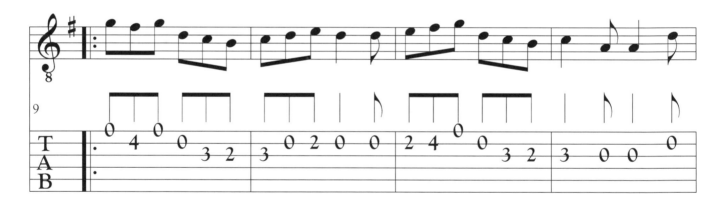

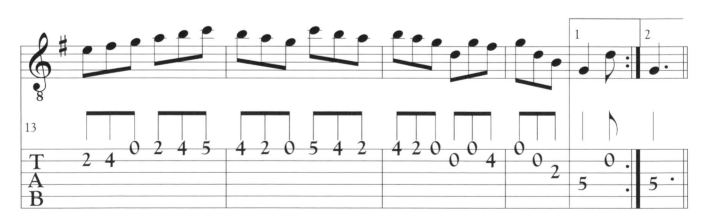

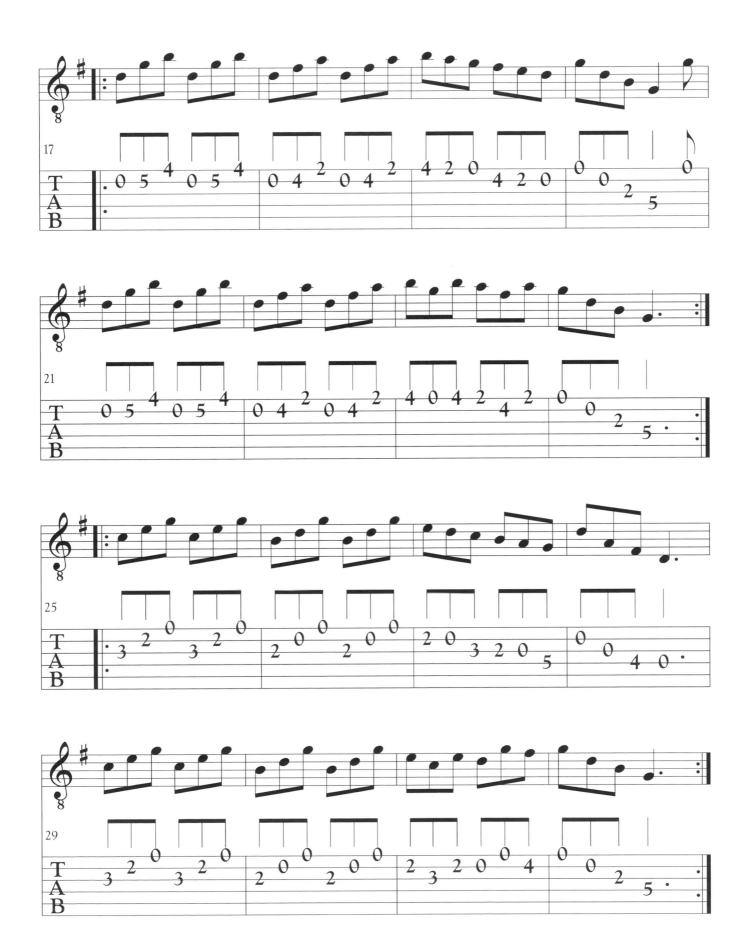

Le Concert ou La Sabatine - Part Two

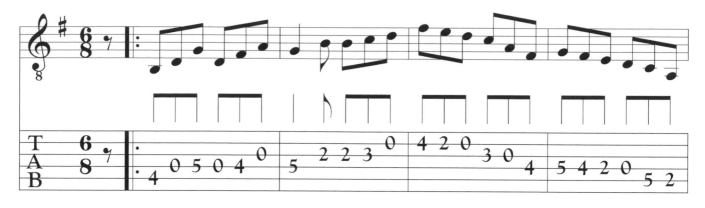

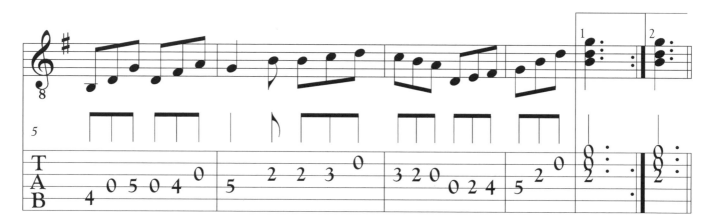

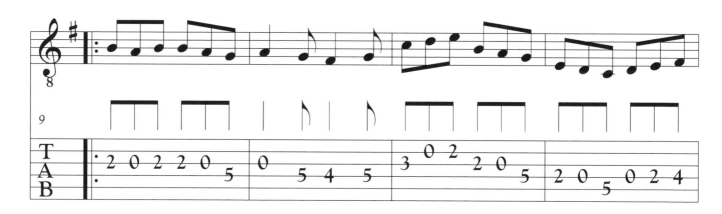

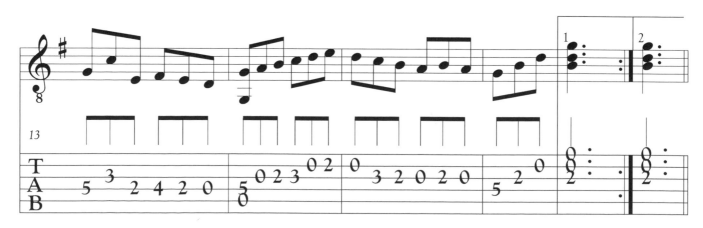

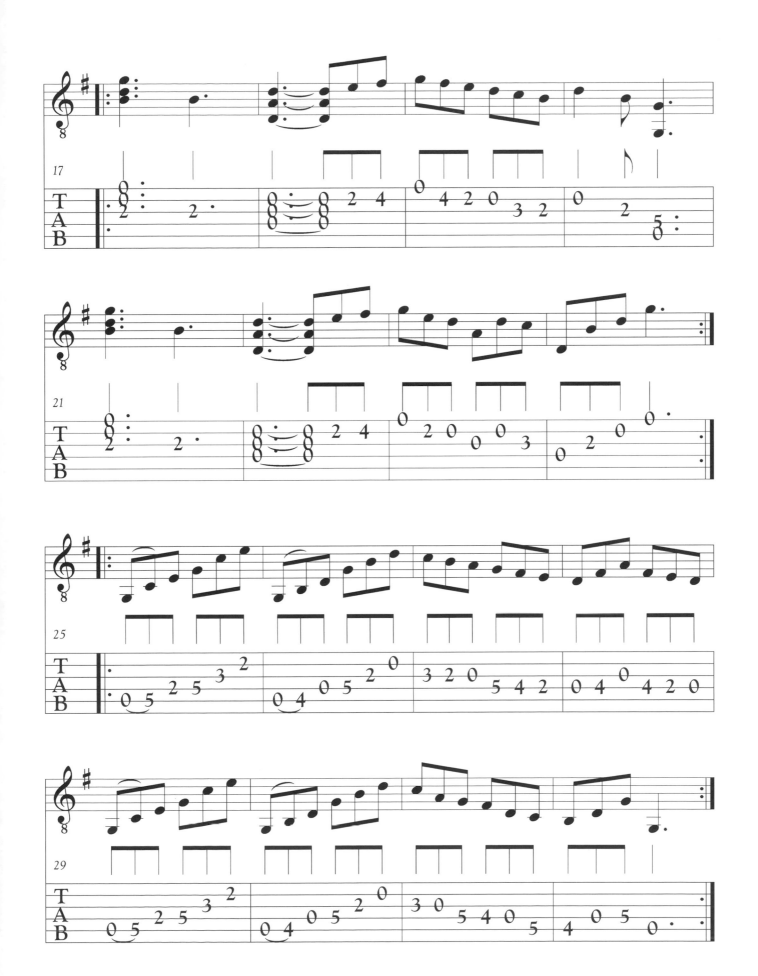

Mantovana - Part One

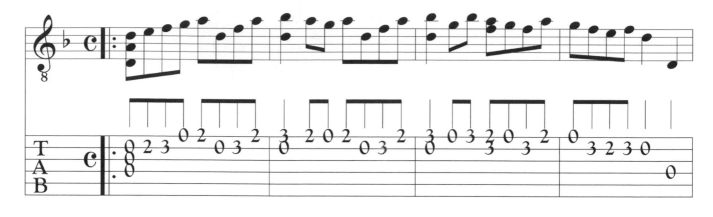

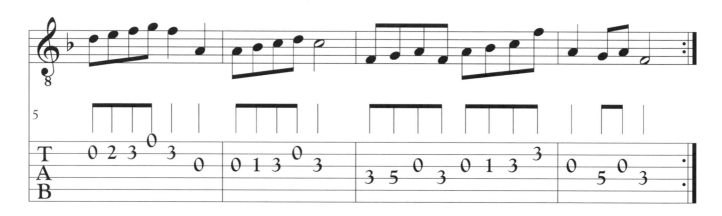

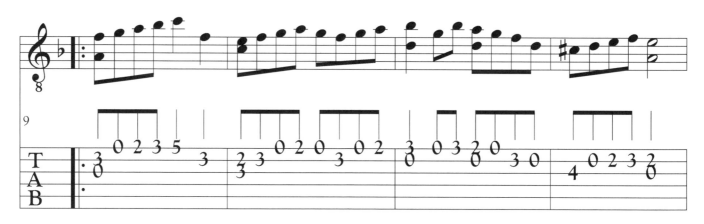

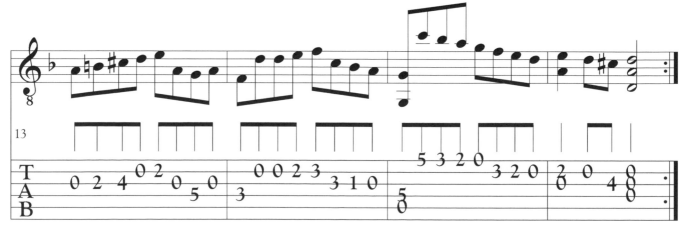

Mantovana - Part Two

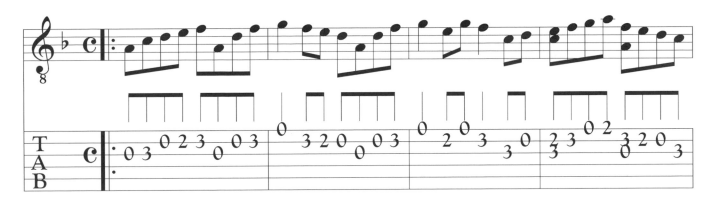

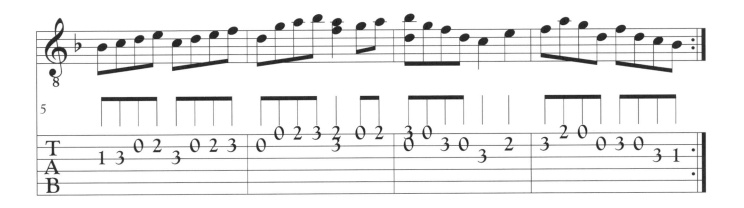

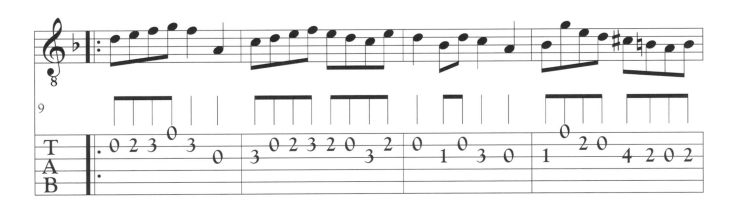

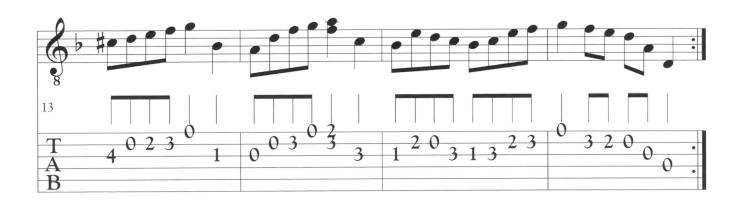

Girandula - Part One

Girandula - Part Two

Common Chord Shapes - Capo Two

D

D
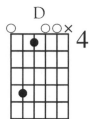

D

D5
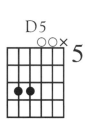

D5
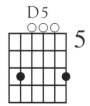

Dm
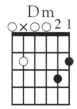

Em

Em
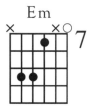

F
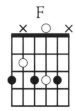

G
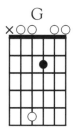

G5

Gm

A
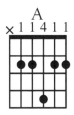

A5
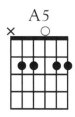

Am
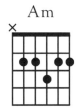

Bm
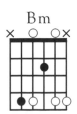

C
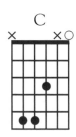

C/G
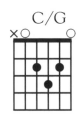

78

CD Tracks

The tunes are played at a medium tempo. I never play a tune the same way twice, but I have tried my best to play as closely as possible to these arrangements. For the pieces in Part One, the basic version is followed by the ornamented version. For the rest of the pieces, variations are played in the repeated sections; for example, A1 is the basic version, A2 is ornamented. Although the tunes are arranged into sets, each tune is played individually.

1. The Peacock's Feather basic version
2. The Peacock's Feather with ornaments
3. The Fairies' Hornpipe basic version
4. The Fairies' Hornpipe with ornaments
5. The Humours of Kilcogher basic version
6. The Humours of Kilcogher with ornaments
7. The Cordal Jig basic version
8. The Cordal Jig with ornaments
9. The Long Note basic version
10. The Long Note with ornaments
11. Rodney's Glory basic version
12. Rodney's Glory with ornaments
13. Brian O'Lynn
14. A Trip to Athlone
15. The Mist Covered Mountain
16. The Mooncoin Jig
17. The Lark in the Morning
18. The Swallow Tail Jig
19. The Banks of Lough Gowna
20. An Phis Fhliuch
21. Poll Ha'penny
22. The Princess Royal
23. The Blackbird
24. The Cliff
25. The Galway
26. The Greencastle
27. The Greencastle Alternate B
28. The Liverpool Hornpipe
29. The Flowers of Edinburgh
30. The Flowers of Michigan
31. The Temperance Reel
32. The Woman of the House
33. The Virginia
34. The Log Cabin
35. The Traveler's Reel
36. The Scholar
37. The Scholar Alternate B
38. Miss Thorton's
39. Miss Thorton's Alternate B
40. La Cardeuse & Le Triomphe
41. La Cardeuse & Le Triomphe Alternate B
42. Jockey to the Fair
43. The Flaxley Green Dance
44. Tom Jones
45. Foul Weather Call
46. The Dorsetshire Hornpipe
47. Polly Put the Kettle On
48. Le Concert ou La Sabatine Melody
49. Le Concert ou La Sabatine Harmony
50. Le Concert ou La Sabatine Duet
51. The Mantovana Melody
52. The Mantovana Harmony
53. The Mantovana Duet
54. Girandula Melody
55. Girandula Harmony
56. Girandula Duet

Special thanks to piper and pipe maker Didier Heuline
for the loan of his 2006 George Lowden F35.

Please visit my websites if you need to contact me -

myspace.com/docrossi
myspace.com/bucheronnegalante
myspace.com/lesdexters
cittern.ning.com

More Great Guitar Books from Centerstream...